HAL•LEONARD®
VIOLIN
PLAY-ALONG

AUDIO
ACCESS
INCLUDED

AndrewLloydWebber™

HITS

Andrew Lloyd Webber™ is a trademark owned by Andrew Lloyd Webber.

The musical works contained in this edition may not be publicly performed in a dramatic form or context except under license from The Really Useful Group Limited, 17 Slingsby Place, London WC2E 9AB

PLAYBACK+
Speed • Pitch • Balance • Loop

To access audio visit:
www.halleonard.com/mylibrary

Enter Code
8667-9693-9861-5353

ISBN 978-1-5400-0309-6

Jon Vriesacker, violin
Audio arrangements by Peter Deneff
Recorded and Produced by Jake Johnson
at Paradyme Productions

HAL•LEONARD®

7777 W. BLUEMOUND RD. P.O. BOX 13819 MILWAUKEE, WI 53213

In Australia Contact:
Hal Leonard Australia Pty. Ltd.
4 Lentara Court
Cheltenham, Victoria, 3192 Australia
Email: ausadmin@halleonard.com.au

Visit Hal Leonard Online at
www.halleonard.com

As If We Never Said Goodbye

from SUNSET BOULEVARD

Music by Andrew Lloyd Webber
Lyrics by Don Black and Christopher Hampton,
with contributions by Amy Powers

Close Every Door

from JOSEPH AND THE AMAZING TECHNICOLOR® DREAMCOAT

Music by Andrew Lloyd Webber
Lyrics by Tim Rice

I Believe My Heart

from THE WOMAN IN WHITE
Music by Andrew Lloyd Webber
Lyrics by David Zippel

I Don't Know How to Love Him

from JESUS CHRIST SUPERSTAR

Words by Tim Rice
Music by Andrew Lloyd Webber

If Only You Would Listen

from SCHOOL OF ROCK

Music by Andrew Lloyd Webber
Lyrics by Glenn Slater

rall.

Love Changes Everything

from ASPECTS OF LOVE
Music by Andrew Lloyd Webber
Lyrics by Don Black and Charles Hart

Think of Me

from THE PHANTOM OF THE OPERA

Music by Andrew Lloyd Webber
Lyrics by Charles Hart
Additional Lyrics by Richard Stilgoe

'Til I Hear You Sing

from LOVE NEVER DIES

Music by Andrew Lloyd Webber
Lyrics by Glenn Slater